MW00679478

We've done it again.

And how could we not? Sales of the first two Vent books — **The Vent: The Book** and **The Vent: Book Deux** — are still lining our pockets, still paying for our kids' braces, still earning obscenely high interest in offshore accounts.

And if you buy that, we've got something *else* to sell you.

In fact, publication of a new Vent book has become a year-ending tradition at the old Journaltution. Why, if we didn't publish **The Vent III,** the year would never end. Think of the chaos, the tumult, the computer crashes. On the other hand, think of the tax benefits, the ability to return dreadful Christmas gifts forever.

OK, so we're publishing **The Vent III** anyway. And we have you to thank for it. You called our anonymous Vent line, and we printed what you said. So thanks!

Who's responsible for this?

Joey Ledford, the Vent Guy and also the paper's Lane Ranger traffic columnist (aka the Dent Guy), that's who. Joey edited this book, and if he wrote a camping column, he'd be the Tent Guy.

Richard Halicks designed and produced this slim tome, his weekly wage having been made contingent upon it.

Hyde Post, our founder and always decorous leader, quite skillfully told people what to do and, in his spare moments, saved France.

John Amoss, creator of the now priceless Vent image, which may be acquired by the Guggenheim (or the Vatican) at any time, did the cover of the book and the illustrations on each title page.

Jim Smith (not his real name) copy edited the book with his usual admirable skill.

When in the Course of Human eVents . . .

It may be that your sole purpose in life is simply to serve as a warning to others.

So many idiots, so few comets.

My father refers to that morning talk show as "Regis and Butthead."

Before you criticize someone,
you should walk a mile in their shoes.
Then, after you criticize them,
you will be a mile away
and you will have their shoes.

All those who believe in psychokinesis,
raise my hand.

At my office, we celebrate Earth Week
and Secretaries Day at the same time.
We treat the secretaries like dirt!

I hate leaving a smoke-free building.
The first thing you smell is 114 cigarettes.

Always smoke brand-name cigarettes.
That way, your family will know who to sue
when you die.

A jury: Twelve people chosen to decide
who has the best lawyer.

I know the real name of Planet Radio's
home world — Ineptune!

Some mornings it's just not worth
chewing through the leather straps.

Elvis was treated like a dog.

They called him King

and then they buried him

in the back yard.

Boys will be boys these days and so will girls.

A new invention for people
who like peace and quiet: A phoneless cord.

Forget "No Smoking" sections in restaurants.
I want to know where the
"No Clapping and Singing 'Happy Birthday' Off-key"
section is.

Shin: A device for finding furniture in the dark.

While paying for dinner at Chick-fil-A,
my wife commented that the cows in the poster
had misspelled chicken.
The teen cashier said,
"I don't think those cows really wrote that.
I think it's just an advertising piece."

I am sick and tired of men downtown
asking me for money. Especially quarters.

It must be true, men are from Mars.
Look at how the place is decorated.

I called my local cable company to complain
about my service and the guy told me
to "turn the TV off and read a book."

Deja Moo:
The feeling that you've heard this bull before.

You know you've had a busy week
when it's Friday and you still have
your Monday panties on.

Congratulations to the FBI.
I heard they were three leads away
from solving the Omni bombing.

I gave up drugs 20 years ago,
but I just can't kick ice cream.

My son received his first paycheck yesterday
and he wants to know who FICA is.

UPS went out on strike. No one could deliver.
I went in for a heart transplant.
Instead I got a liver.

My brother-in-law is so dumb,
he thinks a line-item veto
is a bookkeeper for the Mafia.

My boss asked me if I told anyone about my raise. I told him, "Don't worry, I'm just as ashamed of it as you are."

Did ancient Roman paramedics refer to IVs as fours?

I just took a course on the nuts and bolts
of my job and now I'm not sure
if I'm the nut or the bolt.

It's an old modeling trick:
Wear really big shoes and it makes
your legs look thinner. Note to heavy women:
Don't try this, or you will look like
two tugs trying to pull a ship off a rock.

I still think the Vent
is a government-sponsored
artificial intelligence experiment.

My next-door neighbor is depriving
some small village somewhere of its idiot.

I'm tired of the five-day forecast
in the paper changing every day.

We could have all enjoyed the movie
if you'd left your baby at home with a bottle
and just brought your breasts to the show.

My 4-year-old granddaughter learns fast.
When her brother was teasing
and tormenting her, she raised her hand
and said, "Stop the violence."

When you flip people off in traffic,
I hope it makes you feel better,
because it makes you look really, really dumb.
P.S. Get your roots done.

The statement from my doctor
for a breast examination
included a $5 handling charge.

The two biggest problems

in America are

making ends meet

and making meetings end.

If God had intended for Stone Mountain
to be another Dollywood,
He would have put up
two mounds instead of one.

My boss fired me after he spied
on my office e-mail.
Now I'm at home on my own computer
and I can insult that pig with impunity.

I have been collecting my daylight savings
in little clear jars to use
when we go back on regular time.

My neighbor said he puts cow manure
on his strawberries.
Personally, I like sugar and cream on mine.

Television is so educational.
Until last week I thought paparazzi
was an Italian tenor.

If you hook a dog leash over a ceiling fan,
the motor is not strong enough
to rotate a 42-pound boy
wearing underwear and a Superman cape.

I used to work at the Waffle House.
It was always a dream of mine and I made it happen.

I'd kill for a Nobel Peace Prize.

Unrequited Vent

My teeth are capped. I have breast implants.
My face is lifted. I had a nose job.
My tummy is tucked. My nails are plastic.
I wear contact lenses.
My hair is straightened and tinted.
I wear shoulder pads and high heels.
My makeup is impeccable.
I'm wearing imitation designer clothes.
So now I'm ready to go out on a date
and share the real me with someone special.

Heard on Channel 11:
"Are some women allergic to sex at 11?"
I guess they prefer sex earlier in the evening.

My girlfriend made me
get a dead raccoon out of the road
and bury it.
I sure hope nobody runs over a buffalo.

Hey, Ellen, guess what?
We already knew.

As a guy, I don't see the big deal
about Ellen's big episode.
I would have gone for Laura Dern
over that guy, too!

My wife said she had her hair teased.
To me it looked like it was insulted.

My girlfriend was in the beauty shop
the other day for six hours
and that was just for an estimate.

I hear the Army is changing its slogan
from "Be all you can be"
to "Do everyone you can do."

With all of the sexual activity going on
in the military I bet our president
wonders why he ever dodged the draft.

The cookbook in our house

was written

by Stephen King.

The average woman would rather have beauty
than brains, because the average man
can see better than he can think.

National Condom Week is coming pretty soon
and that's something I don't want to miss.

My doctor asked me if I was sexually active.
I told him no, I just lie there.

Men and computers are alike.
You have to turn them on
to get them to do anything.

You know your marriage is in trouble
when you keep looking at your husband
through the tines of your fork,
so you can imagine what
he would look like in prison.

My brother's wife left him.
She said she had to go find herself.
Heck, if he had known that,
he could have bought her a belt
with her name on it.

I was in line at the bank the other day
and the lady in front of me had a tag on her jeans
that said, "Guess."
I said size 16. Boy, was she mad.

Forest Park has designated 320 acres
on the parkway for adult businesses.
I guess they are going to call this Sex Flags.

You might be a redneck if you refer
to your wife's birthday as her born-on date.

Since my old lady left me,
I have lost my will to drink.

I did an unbelievable amount of work
in the yard. It's amazing what you can do
when your wife puts your mind to it.

After investing 24 years of assets
into a low-interest relationship,
I am considering filing for emotional bankruptcy.

I used to know a lot of blondes
but they all dyed.

Liquor manufacturers should put this label
on their bottles: "Warning: this beverage
can make members of the opposite sex
look more attractive than they are."

Seen on a bumper sticker:
"I still miss my ex-wife
but my aim's getting better."

I'm 60, single and looking for my Martha Stewart,
but everytime the doorbell rings,
it is Lotta Mae with another tuna casserole.

How do I tell my 60-year-old single dad
that he should be looking for Betty Crocker,
not Martha Stewart?

Son, I'm not looking for Martha Stewart
or Betty Crocker.
I'm looking for Sharon Stone.

My wife can't take a compliment.

I told her she looks like

Marilyn Monroe, and she asked,

"Then or now?"

I told my wife the neighbor lady
said she was too old to be cutting the grass.
I haven't had to touch the lawn mower since.

Someone please tell my wife
that in the "just say no" commercial,
they are talking about drugs.

If you think your wife is not much of a cook,
get this. My wife invited everyone over
for the annual lighting of the stove.

I don't think that Upton's girl is so hot.
Her mouth's too big, she's too thin,
her hair's too short, she doesn't have my
phone number and I don't know her name.

Aunt Bee once told Andy he was spending
too much time with Barney.

It's been over a year since I've had a date.
I've gotten so desperate that I've even lowered
the standards in my fantasies.

An insurance agent called and wanted to know
if I have dedicated life.
I said, "Shoot, I don't even have a dedicated wife."

I'm gay but I'd jump ship for Aunt Fritzi.

Being able to hit the snooze button
in the morning is better than sex.

I think it's better to hit the snooze button
and then have sex.

To the snooze button person:
Trust me, you're doing something wrong.

The perfect wife would be a sex-starved beauty who has a million dollars and owns a liquor store.

The perfect husband is one who's 102 years old and has $150 million.

If diamonds are a girl's best friend and dogs are a man's best friend, then why doesn't a woman give a man a dog when they are engaged?

Never mind Mars and Venus.
Men are from Playboy,
women are from Good Housekeeping.

Men are from ESPN,
and women are from Lifetime.

Men are from Mars, women are from Venus,
dogs are from Pluto
and cars are from Saturn and Mercury.

A woman asked her husband,
"Honey, if I die would you let your next wife
use my golf clubs?"
"No," he replied. "She's left-handed."

My wife is just wonderful.
She brings in the mail and newspaper,
cuts the grass, and, in addition,
is small and cheap to feed.

I heard there are more women than men in heaven because men won't ask for directions.

I was humming an old song and my younger
friend said, "Stop, you're dating yourself."
I replied, "No way.
Dating yourself could lead to incest."

My wife and I enjoy our new hobby so much
we're having her move in with us.

If Hooters has to hire more men,
it's time to change its name to Hooters and Shooters.

I noticed TBS is showing "Thelma and Louise."
Is this a new series,
"Movies for Women Who Hate Guys?"

I would marry Aunt Fritzi tomorrow
except I know she would want to bring
Nancy on our honeymoon.

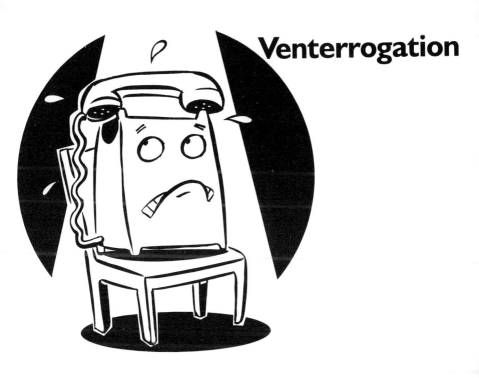

Venterrogation

Why do people always say,
"On a scale from one to 10,
with 10 being the highest . . ."?
What else is 10 going to be?

Why is it that for the first two years of a child's life
we try to get them to walk and talk,
and for the next 16 to 18 years
we try to get them to sit down and shut up?

The government is storing fingerprints
in a digital format?
What other format
could they be stored in?

If Kroger is now a verb — Go Krogering —
can we also say "He Krogered it"
or "Man, I was really Krogered last night?"

If you beep somebody
and their beeper is not on,
where does the beep go?

Anyone knows if you beep someone
and the beeper isn't on,
the beep goes on.

What's a dyslexic agnostic with insomnia?
A person who lays awake at night
wondering whether there's a dog.

Early to bed, and early to rise,
do you make enough cash to do otherwise?

Is George Clooney Rosemary's baby?

What are we gonna party like
when it actually *is* 1999?

When a man is retiring, why does
his company always give him a watch?
The time is the last thing
he wants to keep up with.

I understand May is breast-feeding month in Georgia.
What do they eat, anyway?

Have you ever seen

a Persian rug

that wasn't on sale?

Do fire ants drive little red trucks?

If fire ants drive red Matchbox trucks,
do carpenter ants wear those little tool belts?

Are soldier ants allowed to carry weapons?

Did Agent Scully have to take a special class at the FBI academy to learn how to chase criminals in high heels?

Does anyone else besides me have paper cuts on the back of their ears from using 3-D glasses?

You read Nancy twice a day and you think *she* is dumb?

If Hillary is convicted and sent to prison,
would she still get Secret Service protection?

Now that the British have vacated Hong Kong,
are they really going to have to wait 30 days
to get their security deposit back?

Why do banks chain down their ink pens?
They never work, so why would you want them?

I notice a lot of people cite
personal and professional reasons for leaving a job.
What other reasons are there?

My son says I need help.
Do you know if there is
a Beanie Babies Anonymous?

Do you think there's any chance
they will name one of the rocks on Mars Izzy?

Why don't they just ask the Olympic bomber to do the Omni and save a lot of money?

If explosives are used for an explosion, why aren't implosives used for an implosion?

I'm starting to get into this imploding thing. What's scheduled for next weekend?

Why is it when something is destroyed
that is man-made it's called vandalism,
but when man destroys something
that God made
it's called development?

If I should die before I wake,
could someone please come dust my house
before the preacher comes?

There's extra small, and there's extra large,
but why isn't there extra medium?

How can you sweep the mess under the rug
when you have wall-to-wall carpet?

How can they give an Oscar for editing?
Isn't that the part of the movie we didn't see?

When you show someone a picture of you
and they say, "Wow, that's a good picture!"
is that a compliment or an insult?
Isn't it like saying,
"Wow, you are much uglier than that!"

PhD stands for Post Hole Digger, right?

Why is it that people say they can kill two birds
with one stone, but you never see the dead birds?

Have you ever wondered why,
when Superman flew over,
there was never any sonic boom?

Since they put pictures of missing children
on milk cartons, why don't they put pictures
of fugitives on beer cans?

About a bird in hand being messy,
did you know the messy part of the bird
is called the vent?

Do windbreakers
really break wind?

Have you ever imagined a world
with no hypothetical situations?

Does anybody else out there think those aliens
in "The X-Files"
look a little too much like Ross Perot?

Why won't TV newscasters just tell us
what they want to tell us instead of telling us
that they're going to tell us
what they want to tell us?

Is it just me or does Ken Cook
look like a member of that Duracell battery family?

You never said. Is it illegal to hide
a dead body for your girlfriend?

Is there still time to get breast implants
and get in on that settlement?

How can a radio station have an exclusive
Weather Channel forecast?
Didn't the Weather Channel have it first?

Now that you've got the Rush Hour Recap,
what's next? Yesterday's Weather?

When lobsters are
"gently steamed to perfection,"
does that mean they don't feel the pain?

When a woman has a baby,
how come people bring her a balloon
with "It's a boy," or "It's a girl" on it?
Doesn't she already know?

That ugly tower next to the Varsity
was supposed to be an Olympic flame?
I always thought is was the
Dairy Queen Memorial.

I went to get my driver's license renewed
and the examiner asked me,
"Are you still a veteran?"

Can you believe Grady Hospital is building
a smoker's pavilion next to the cardiac-care unit?
What's next? An adult novelty shop
near the maternity ward?

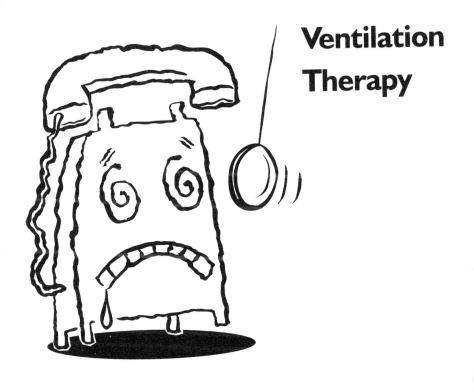

Ventilation Therapy

I never go outside 285. I've seen "Deliverance."

I don't go inside 285. I've seen "Pulp Fiction."

I live inside 285 — just me and my machine gun.

I don't go outside 285
because I know what they do to traffic lights.

Seen in the classifieds:
"Dog for sale.
Eats anything and loves children."

They should make duct tape in many colors,
so I could repair my carpet.

The sign says, "Ears pierced while you wait."
Darn! I wanted to leave them
and pick them up later.

Wear comfortable shoes at the Arts Festival:
Hell hath no fury like a woman's corns.

When our plane arrived late,
the Delta pilot said over the PA,
"We apologize for your patience."
I thought, "That's OK. We appreciate the delay."

My niece came home from school
and told her mom the nurse had to check
everyone's hair for head lights.

Everybody should believe in something.
I believe I'll have another beer!

The further you go, the meaner they get
and I live in the last house on the left.

Some of the Freaknik celebrants missed their Sunday flights because of traffic jams. Now that's justice.

They say that drinking water prevents stiffness in joints. The problem is they don't serve water in a lot of joints.

So Luke Skywalker lands on this planet, and he needs training in using the Force, and Yoda Yoda Yoda, he's a Jedi Knight.

I need to go

to a rehab center

because I'm

hooked on phonics.

Don't wear flip-flops
on the new Batman ride at Six Flags.

Clothes make the man. Naked people
have little or no influence on society.

Naked people have no influence on society?
Without the cooperative efforts of naked people
in groups of two there would be no society.

Not many people know that the reason
they call the guy who wrote "The Odyssey" Homer
is because he wore his baseball cap backwards.

If Homer wrote "The Odyssey,"
did Jethro draw the illustrations?

Homer is not just a mascot and an author
of classic epics. He also has a lucrative endorsement
contract with Home Depot.

My husband is so smart he can bounce
the remote signal off the fireplace
and change TV channels.

Explain to me one more time
how I can borrow my way out of debt.
I keep forgetting.

You might be a Peachtree City redneck
if you have a golf cart up on blocks
in your front yard.

NASA says that rover is female,
but I don't believe it.
I saw it lift its leg against that big rock.

Did you ever wonder why smokers drive
with their windows open?
Maybe they are worried about
the effects of second-hand smoke.

I was just in downtown Atlanta for a convention,
and it looks like the bomber got the Omni
and Atlanta-Fulton County Stadium.
I sure hope they get this guy soon.

We ran out of fax paper and our secretary
didn't want to drive in all that rain
so she called the supply company
and asked them to just fax over some more paper.

Sure, we could start making fun of Alabama,
but where's the challenge?

Order pizza from your car phone,
outrun the pizza guy for 30 minutes
and your pizza is free!

I stopped at a store yesterday
and bought a candy bar and a Coke.
The man asked me if I had gotten gas.
I said, "No, but I will when I finish this."

Barbie is just like new Coke.
Once they realize you can't mess
with perfection, they'll leave it alone.

One advantage to being stupid
is that you never get lonely.

Police station toilet seat stolen.

Cops have nothing to go on.

Let's see now, Madonna is a mother,
Michael Jackson is a father-to-be
and the artist formerly known as Prince and his wife
are reportedly brand-new parents.
Hmm, PTA meetings should be very interesting
a few years from now.

I think Underground Atlanta
needs a Wal-Mart.

If we could just get everyone to close their eyes
and visualize world peace for an hour,
imagine how serene and quiet it would be
until the looting started.

A day without sunshine is like,
you know, night.

While talking to my students
about what Memorial Day means to them,
one proudly announced that his father
fought in a war,
"and he would be dead if he hadn't survived."

I was looking at the pictures
of the Martian landscape
and I believe I saw a fire ant mound.

Just for today, I will not sit in my living room
all day watching TV.
Instead, I will move my TV
into the bedroom.

I've eaten the same overprocessed cat food
year after year, and I feel perfectly healthy.

I've been answering the doorbell
for the last month and a half in nothing but a towel
hoping that it would be
the Publishers Clearinghouse Prize Patrol.

This just in: The FBI has strong evidence
that the Omni and stadium explosions
may be the work of the same bomber.

My 3-year-old niece's new pediatrician
walked into the room with his bright red hair,
freckles and glasses, and she exclaimed,
"I want to look just like you for Halloween."

I am so bored with my job
that I started working on a book,
and if this one turns out OK,
I may start reading another one.

If more people
were like Xena the Warrior Princess,
crime in Atlanta would probably
be way, way down.

I'm really busy so I only read
the two- and three-line vents.

Power corrupts,

but absolute power

is kind of neat.

There's a bum in Centennial Park.
You have 30 minutes before
he approaches you
and asks for spare change.

This is area code 770 speaking.
Surrender, 404, we've got you surrounded.

Newsweek has named Bill Campbell
as one of our National Mayors to Watch.
I think 24-hour surveillance
would be a very good idea.

So City Council is going to fine the homeless
$1,000 for urban camping.
If they had $1,000,
they'd be staying at the Ritz-Carlton.

Game Face Vent

My horse came in 20 to 1.
Unfortunately, the race started at 12:30.

I saw the Kentucky Derby on TV.
It was kind of like having sex.
They talked for an hour,
then they had two minutes of action.

Will Rogers never met Mark Bradley.

I heard that the newborn son of Braves' pitcher
Greg Maddux is going to be named Chase.
With the money that Greg has,
the kid's middle name should be "Manhattan."

It's I before E, except after C and,
of course, after W in Budweiser.

It's comforting to know that Vince Dooley
took the advice of a 5-year-old.
Congratulations to UGA's new basketball coach.
What was his name again? Barney?

Somebody please explain to me
how they can pay a guy millions
to play baseball
and still have to give him
$50 a day for meal money?

Let's bring O.J. Simpson
back to Monday Night Football.
He can team with Frank Gifford
and we can call them
"the Cheater and the Beater."

Sports trivia: Who is the oldest man
to win the Heisman Trophy?
Fred Goldman.

Chipper Jones needs to change his name to the more appropriate Dipper Jones.

Does Chipper Jones buy his sunflower seeds at the ballpark or does he sneak them in?

Could we name the new Atlanta hockey team "The Freeze?" That way we can sing, "O'er the land of the Freeze, and the home of the Braves!"

Mike Tyson:

If you can't beat 'em,

eat 'em.

I was going to contribute to the United Way,
but I decided to use the money to play golf
at Callaway Gardens
and cut out the middle man.

You have to hand it to the Falcons.
They've done a terrific job
switching to the no-run, no-shoot offense.

When I win the lottery,
I am going to buy two hot dogs
and a Coke at Turner Field.

Everyone is taking credit for getting
the Braves to reverse the food policy,
but we Venters know the truth.

A discovery made before the food policy changed:
M&M's won't melt in your bra, either.

Why they keep calling Randy Johnson
the Big Unit? How do they know?

The new Mike Tyson Computer:
Two bites and no memory.

One tequila, two tequila, three tequila, floor.

Enough of the cookbook —
the next Braves Wives' publication
I want to see is, "How to Bag a Brave."

I believe one day Terence Moore
will write something that makes sense.

One of the Falcons' new players said he thinks
he can turn the secondary around.
So that's why they've been so bad!

You definitely have too much time
on your hands if you drive to Chattanooga
to see a Falcons scrimmage.

I tried to make my BellSouth call
to the Braves' bullpen but it didn't work.
Evidently, Bobby Cox's calls
haven't worked either.
Maybe he should try MCI.

Swimming is the perfect exercise.
You don't get dirty when you do it,
you're clean when you're done
and you get to watch everybody else
wearing a bathing suit.

After I eat one of those wide-mouth bass,
I can't eat a regular bass anymore
because I don't get anything out of it.

The Falcons are like a fine wine
— lying down in the cellar.

John Smoltz now has enough money
to buy the sun and position it wherever he wants
for maximum pool coverage.

I see Andre Rison has changed jobs again.
Think about what he must spend on resumes.

Reinstate Pete Rose?

You bet.

Chicken wings is one of the four major
TV sports food groups —
along with beer, pizza and doughnuts.

I moved to Atlanta to get as far as I could
from professional football and then, darn it,
they put a team in Jacksonville.

Stop calling Turner Field "the Ted."
It sounds like a gay bar.

It's a good thing the Braves
got the new stadium for free.
Imagine how much everything would cost
if they were paying for it.

Ventura Highway

The reason the Russian space station
keeps hitting or just missing other spacecraft
is that objects in Mir are closer than they appear.

I just bought a used UPS truck,
which you may not think is very cool,
but at least I can park anywhere I want.

If I enter an elevator and my floor is pushed,
I always push it again
because I know I'm a better driver.

If you were going the speed of light
on the way to work, time would stop,
you'd have infinite mass and zero volume.
So even if you did make it in,
you'd be late, heavy and pointless.

I ran over one of them speed bumps
real quick with my truck and darn near
knocked my spit cup all over my boots.
That's why we go slow over them.

I bought my wife a car
and she told me it leaked.
I said, "Where is the car?"
She said, "In the lake."

Anybody who drives on Ga. 400
knows that there are aliens in Roswell.

I told my boss I was late for work
this morning because of the time disturbance
known as El Moonyo.

Planet Radio is dead in the water.
Now it's time for another alien autopsy.

You know you are having a bad day
when you pull up at a red light
behind a motorcycle gang,
and when the light changes,
your horn gets stuck.

The picture on my driver's license looks great,
but of course my license is about to expire.

Far-Vent-nu-gin.

DOT:

Drunk On Tar.

My wife ran out of gas.
She said she was too busy driving
to stop and buy it.

Instead of telling everybody
I was going to the hospital for a colonoscopy,
I said I was getting an emission inspection.

At Six Flags, I got to ride the Ninja twice
without getting off — I called it deja wooooo.

Now that we have a vehicle on Mars,
for goodness sake,
let's keep a close eye on Wayne Shackelford.

My brother-in-law is a real go-getter.
Every morning he takes his wife to work,
every afternoon he goes and gets her.

Overheard in traffic court:
"How far apart were the cars
when the collision occurred?"

It amazes me how squirrels
can run through the trees
without poking their little eyes out.

It was really good to see people hugging,
kissing and crying as they said goodbye
to their suitcases forever at Hartsfield.

I stopped at a red light and this lady
came up to my car
and said she would do anything for $100.
She is coming over Saturday to paint my house.

Driving alongside 18-wheelers in the rain
on the new and improved Downtown Connector
is like doing the speed limit through a car wash.

I have a friend who's so nervous
he wears his seat belt at a drive-in movie.

When I asked the salesman at the appliance store
why the vacuum cleaner he was showing me
had a headlight, he said it was so I could
see the vacuum if the power went off.

Why do they make you show
your driver's license to get a drink?
Everybody knows you shouldn't drink and drive.

Coming soon to a garage near you
— Emissions: Impossible.

I stopped at a red light and was hit from behind.
The lady said,
"Excuse me, I thought you
were going to run it."

Whenever I start getting sad
about where I am in my life,
I think about the last words
of my favorite uncle:
"A truck!"

What you have to realize is that
on the Georgia license plate when it says,
"Give wildlife a chance,"
what they really mean is give them a running start.

Of course we give wildlife a chance;
a chance to stick its cute little head
out of the bushes before we blow its brains out
and make stew.

I asked my wife why there were so many dings
on the driver's side of her Mercedes
and she said the brakes
must be bad on that side.

A redneck's conception of haute cuisine:
"Red beans and rice
with a garnish of sun-dried roadkill."

Sign seen outside an Auburn residence:
"Datsun puppies for sale."

**Heaven-sent
Vent**

Sign on a Roswell church:
"Don't let worry get you down.
Let the church help."

At the rate we are going,
nobody is going to be around
to cast the first stone.

I heard that a million monkeys
banging on a million typewriters
will eventually reproduce
the entire works of Shakespeare.
Now, thanks to the Internet,
we know this is not true.

Dennis Rodman said he would rather
be a moron than a Mormon.
Did anyone inform him that God
had already granted his wish?

Support Disney:
Boycott the Baptists.

Disney can relax.
The Baptists are also against
drinking, smoking and dancing
and it hasn't hurt those industries.

I'm gay and it's time that I revealed
my shameful, embarrassing secret to the world:
I was raised a Southern Baptist.

After seeing how Disney is doing financially, I was wondering if I could get the Baptists to boycott my company.

Will somebody please tell Channel 5 that it's not Ken Cook's weather. It's God's weather.

No, it is Ken Cook's weather. God is much more accurate.

My home church welcomes all denominations,
but really prefers tens and twenties.

I gave my 4-year-old a dollar
to put in the collection plate at church,
telling her it was for God.
She stuck it in her purse and said,
"OK, I'll give it to him when I see him."

Atheism is a

nonprophet organization.

My 6-year-old son told our preacher
that when he got some money, he was going to
give him some. The preacher said,
"Well, thank you, but why?"
My son replied, "Because my daddy said
you're the poorest preacher we've ever had."

I told my niece I had given up pizza
for Lent. She wanted to know why I would do that
for something out of the dryer.

I went to church Sunday morning
and the preacher said,
"Would someone come and receive the offering?"
A visitor said, "If nobody else will, I will."

For the past year I prayed I'd win the Lotto.
Nothing. Tonight, I prayed, "Why have you failed
me, Lord?" The clouds parted, and a voice
boomed: "Meet me halfway on this. Buy a ticket."

At a recent family reunion,
a cousin told me,
"I used to change your diapers
when you were a baby."
I replied, "Well, you won't recognize the old place.'

A bumper sticker on an Escort read:
"Follow me to Jesus." I followed.
Apparently Jesus lives at a Hooters.

I just want to thank all the cows of the world.
I love milk, I love cheese, I love hamburgers,
I love T-bone steaks, I love filet mignon,
and I love ice cream.
Thank you, cows.

It's hard to fight an enemy
who has an outpost in your head.

There are three stages in life:
Youth, middle age and "you're looking good."

Venta
Claus

It has already been a great Christmas.
I decked the Halls
and then I went next door
and knocked out the Joneses.

We had a successful Christmas family reunion.
There wasn't a single cutting, stabbing or shooting.

How can the Flintstones have a Christmas special when they lived in the B.C. era?

The main reason Santa is so jolly is because he knows where all the bad girls live.

I'm cutting the Vent out of the paper every day and giving it away as Christmas presents.

I don't understand parts of "Silent Night."
For example, what are heavenly peas
and why would anybody
want to sleep in them?

Who is that Round John Virgin guy?

Buying Christmas presents
for my parents is getting very difficult.
They already have every
Jim Nabors record ever made.

I have discovered the true meaning
of Christmas.
It's retail sales.

People wish it was Christmas every day
of the year, but that would mean
I'd have to spend several hours every day
with my crazy sister-in-law.
So I don't think so.

I got a form letter from my sister-in-law
for Christmas, and she misspelled my name.

Only seven

shoplifting days

until Christmas.

I think the hot toy this Christmas
will be the Divorced Barbie.
She will come with all of Ken's stuff.

Help! How can I look like
the Upton's girl by Christmas?

Have you ever noticed that what
was a good present when we were kids
is now called a stocking stuffer?

I won't feel that Christmas is here
until I see that old lady clapping her hands
on TV to turn off the lights.

I'm so glad it's Christmastime again.
I'm going to gun down the Chia pet
with the salad shooter and watch it all
with my snake light.

My family is coming into town for the holidays.
Thank God for Prozac.

I want to know who tangled
those Christmas tree lights
I put away so carefully last year.

This is the time of the year
when we all feel like drug addicts.
We're all going through cold turkey.

This year we're giving blood for Christmas.